The heart

Iain Gilmour and Tony Head

Medical consultant Carol Bryan

This book gives you an introduction to medical studies. You will need to read chapters 1, 2 and perhaps 4 before you can fully understand the later parts of the text.

Contents

1	What is your heart?	2
2	Where is your heart?	4
3	What does your heart look like?	6
4	What does your heart do?	8
5	What is the pulse?	10
6	What are the common heart problems?	12
7	What is a heart attack?	15
8	Heart transplants and pace makers	17
9	Experiments	20
	Glossary	22
	Further information	23
	Index	24

1 What is your heart?

The heart is the pump which pushes blood around the body. The heart is an organ made from a very special kind of muscle.

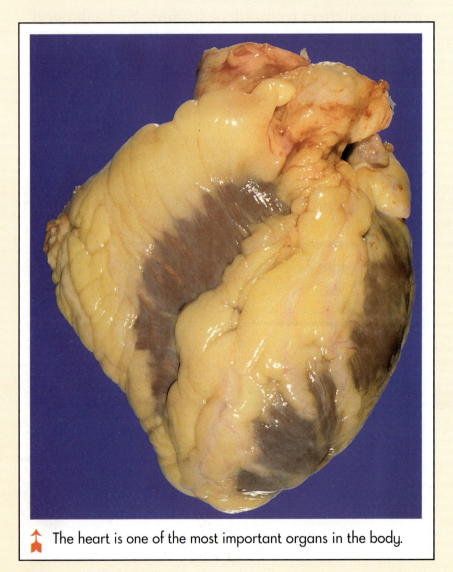

↑ The heart is one of the most important organs in the body.

The heart is one of the major organs in the body. Its job is to push blood around the body. It is an involuntary muscle which works all the time. The brain does not have to think about controlling the heart all the time because it beats involuntarily.

In the past

Over many years, views about what the heart is have changed. The Ancient Greeks believed that the heart was like the brain and that we used the heart to think. Later on, opinions changed and people thought that the heart controlled our emotions. Now modern science has found out what the heart actually is and what it does. However, the fact remains that the heart is one of the most important organs in our body.

Throughout history, people like Aristotle have realised the importance of the heart to life.

2 Where is your heart?

Your heart is inside your rib cage. These bones help keep your heart safe.

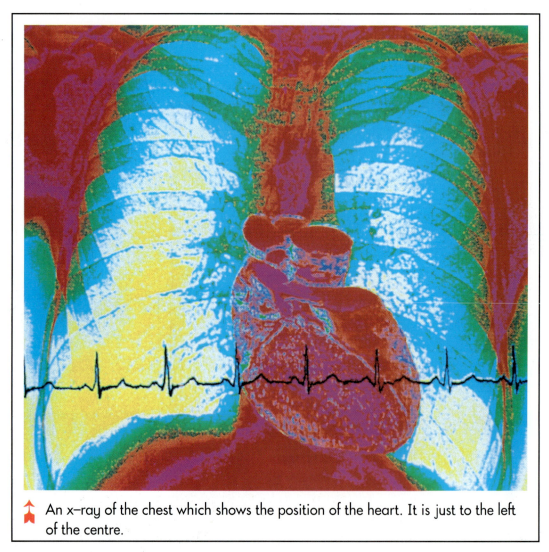

⬆ An x-ray of the chest which shows the position of the heart. It is just to the left of the centre.

Your heart is inside your chest. Your chest is made up of a number of different bones. These bones are the ribs, the breast plate (or sternum) and the backbone. Other organs in your chest are the lungs. The heart is between your lungs and it is protected by the bones of the rib cage and breast plate. The bones and lungs help to keep the heart in the right position.

In more detail

In more detail, the heart is found between your backbone and your sternum which is also known as the breast plate. On each side of the heart are the lungs. These two important organs are protected by the sternum, backbone and rib cage. These bones form the chest cavity.

Try to feel your heart working by pressing your fingers on your rib cage just below your left nipple. You can feel your heart working here because it touches your rib cage.

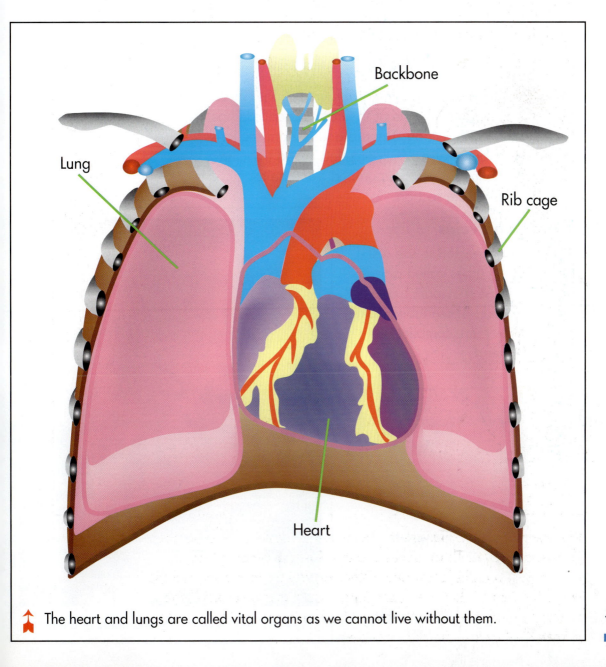

The heart and lungs are called vital organs as we cannot live without them.

3 What does your heart look like?

Your heart is almost the same shape as a love heart. A person's heart is about the same size as their fist.

The inside of the heart is made up of four sections. There are two sections on each side of the heart. Each side has a top and a bottom section. The top and bottom sections are connected by a valve which only lets blood travel in one direction. Blood is always pumped from the top section to the bottom section.

Arteries and veins

The heart is connected to the rest of the body by tubes called arteries and veins. These transport blood around the body. These tubes make the heart look more complicated than a love heart.

Atrium

Ventricle

A drawing showing the chambers of the heart.

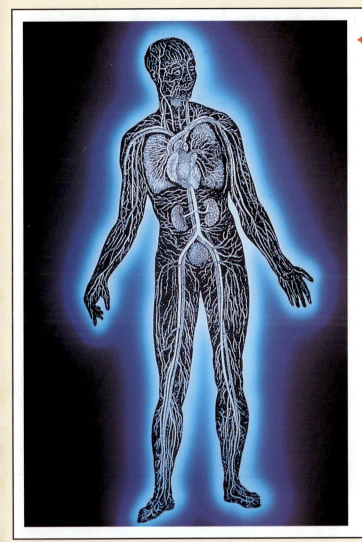

◂ The main veins which take blood to the heart are called the venae cavae. The main artery which takes blood from the heart is the aorta.

The four sections

The four sections of the heart are called chambers. Each chamber has a special name. The top two chambers are called atria which is the plural of atrium. The bottom two chambers are called ventricles. Each side of the heart has an atrium and a ventricle. Each atrium and ventricle is connected by a valve which only lets blood move in one direction. The ventricles are bigger than the atria.

The outside of the heart is covered in a layer of fat. The fat makes a pattern that looks as if the heart has been combed.

There are also extra arteries and veins on the outside of the heart. Arteries supply oxygenated blood to the heart itself. The heart needs this oxygenated blood to make it work as a pump.

4 What does your heart do?

Your heart pushes blood around your body. It does this all the time. If your heart did not pump blood around your body, you would die.

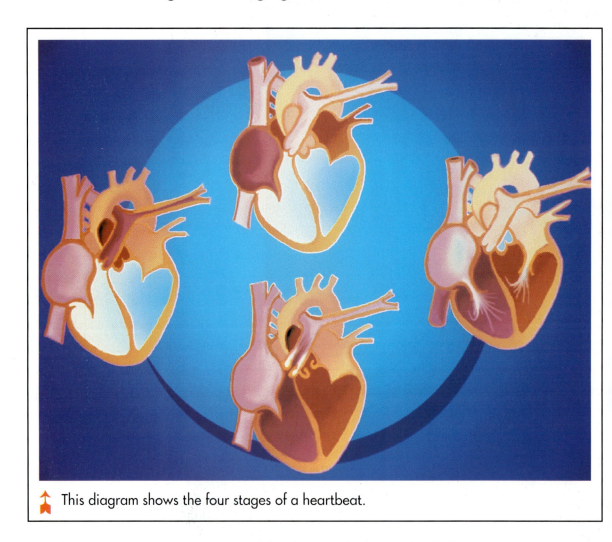

⬆ This diagram shows the four stages of a heartbeat.

Your heart is a pump which pushes blood around your body all the time. This means blood is always moving around your body.

To stay alive, you have to have blood which has oxygen in it. The heart pumps blood to and from the lungs. The lungs put the oxygen that you need to live into the blood.

The importance of oxygen

Your blood never stays still. The blood that the heart pumps around the body has oxygen in it. The body needs this oxygen to work. The speed at which the heart pumps this blood around the body depends on how much oxygen the body needs. When you are exercising, your body needs more oxygen than it does when you are resting so the heart works harder.

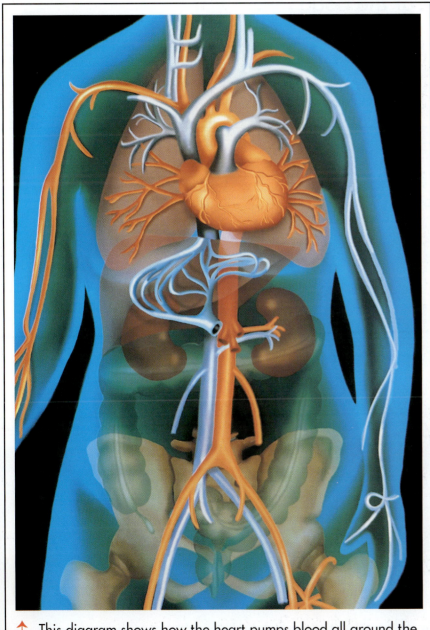

⬆ This diagram shows how the heart pumps blood all around the body.

5 What is the pulse?

The pulse is made when blood moves through the tubes that connect the heart to the rest of the body.

↑ The pulse on the side of the neck is the one first aiders use. It shows whether blood is getting to the brain or not.

The heartbeat

The pulse is made when the arteries which carry the blood push in and out. The arteries are pushed in and out every time the heart beats. We can feel this happening in certain places on the body. These places are where an artery is near to the surface of the skin.

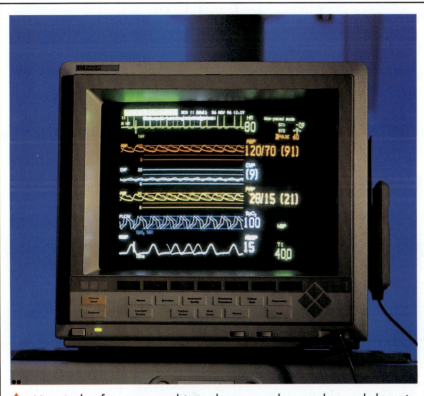

↑ Hospitals often use machines that can take a pulse and show it on a screen.

Feeling your pulse

As the heart pumps blood around the body, the arteries throb at the same time. This makes the pulse. You can feel your pulse by lightly pressing your first two fingers on one side of your throat. You may need to practise this a few times before you can find your pulse.

When somebody has an accident and you cannot feel a pulse, it may mean that their heart is not beating. Find an adult or dial 999 and ask for an ambulance.

11

6 What are the common heart problems?

Not everyone's heart works as it should. Some people are born with something wrong with their heart. Other people get problems as they grow older. The most common heart problems are 'leaky valves' and a 'hole in the heart'.

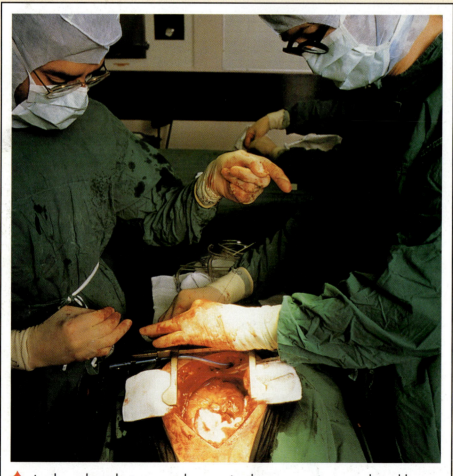

Leaky valves that cannot be repaired are sometimes replaced by artificial valves.

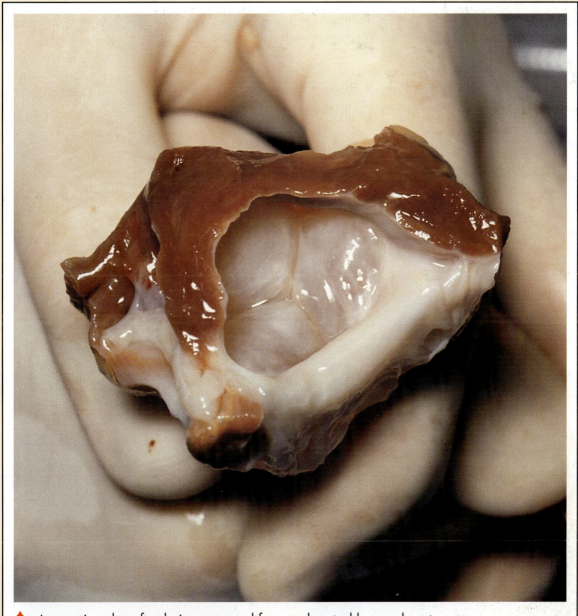

An aortic valve after being removed from a donated human heart.

If the heart has a leaky valve, the blood does not get pushed around the body properly. Some blood leaks back through the one-way valve.

When babies are growing in their mother's womb, the two top chambers in their heart have a hole between them. By the time the baby is born, this hole should be closed up. Sometimes it does not close completely. This is called a hole in the heart.

Leaky valves

Healthy valves only let blood flow in one direction but leaky valves let blood flow either way. This means the amount of oxygenated blood the heart pumps around the body, in one beat, is less than it should be. The heart has to work harder to get oxygen to the body.

Hole in the heart

In a healthy heart, the two upper chambers are separate but when a person has a hole in the heart, these two upper chambers are joined. This causes the heart to have problems.

One of the problems is that blood with too little oxygen in it is allowed to flow back around the body. This is bad for the body. The heart has to work harder to make sure the body gets enough oxygenated blood.

The hole in the heart usually closes as the baby gets older but if this does not happen, an operation is needed to close the hole.

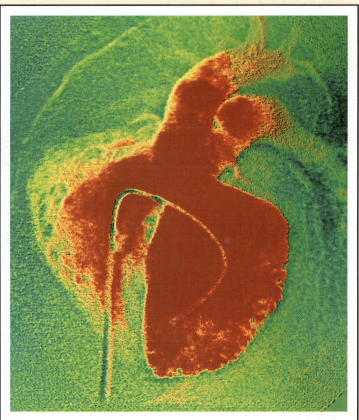

 A hole in the heart will make a person breathless and tired after doing simple things like walking down the street.

7 What is a heart attack?

When the heart suddenly stops beating, it is called a heart attack.

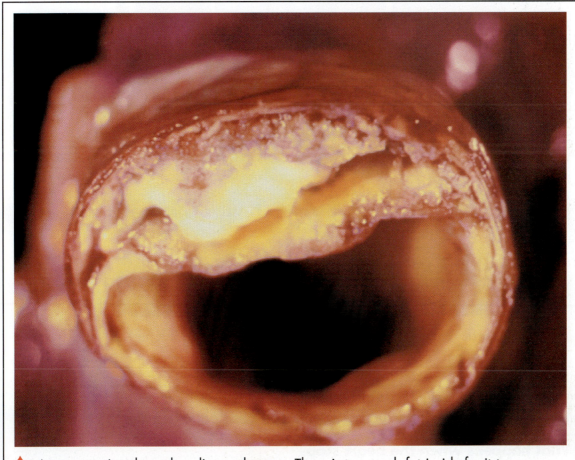

⬆ A cross section through a diseased artery. There is too much fat inside for it to work properly.

A heart attack might happen if an unhealthy heart has been made to work too hard for a long time.

Blocked arteries

Blocked arteries are a sign of an unhealthy heart. Arteries get blocked by an unwanted lining of fat on the inside. They are the main cause of the heart being made to work too hard.

How can you tell if somebody has had a heart attack?

When a person has a heart attack, they look very ill. You cannot feel their heart beating. It has stopped. They have also stopped breathing.

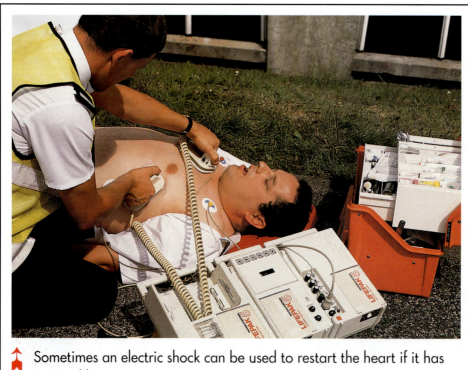

↑ Sometimes an electric shock can be used to restart the heart if it has stopped beating.

When someone suffers a heart attack, their face changes colour and they look very unwell. This is because their heart has stopped beating.

What happens when the heart stops

If a heart stops beating, blood is not pumped around the body. This means that blood, and the oxygen in it, is not getting to the important organs. If an organ does not get oxygen regularly, it will stop working and the person can die.

If someone's heart is not beating, you need to get help fast. Find an adult or dial 999 and ask for an ambulance.

8 Heart transplants and pace makers

Heart transplants

Sometimes a person's heart needs taking out and changing because it is not working properly, or it is unhealthy. When somebody's heart is taken out and changed, it is called a heart transplant.

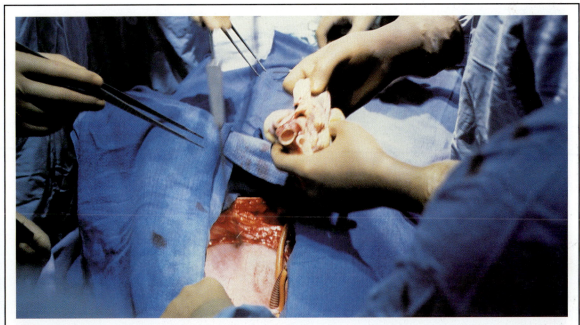

⬆ A heart transplant operation takes many hours to carry out because of the number of arteries and veins that have to be reconnected.

Operations

A heart is transplanted during an operation by skilled surgeons. The heart which needs replacing is taken out of the body, then a new heart is put in. This operation is very difficult and takes many hours to do. After a time, the new heart will often make the person feel more healthy.

When somebody dies in an accident, their heart can sometimes be given to an ill person. Some people carry a card which says that they do not mind their heart being used after they are dead. This card is called a donor card.

A heart transplant takes a long time to do because all the veins and arteries have to be cut from the old heart, and attached to the new one. All these tubes are sewn together by the surgeon. The surgeon makes sure the veins and arteries are in the right place.

Pace makers

A healthy heart beats all the time. Some hearts miss a beat when a person is not healthy. A pace maker stops the heart from missing any beats.

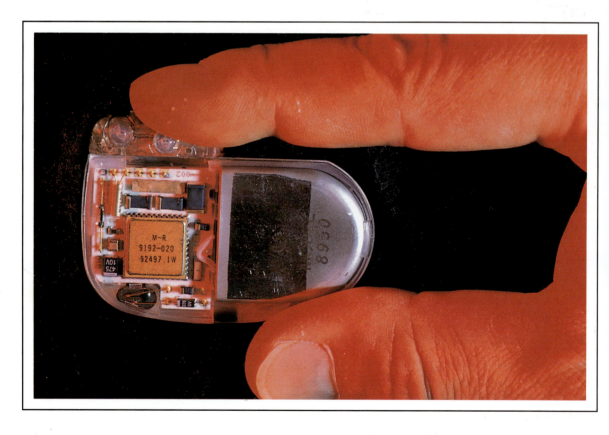

A pace maker is a small, metal, electrical device which is linked to the heart. It helps to keep the heart beating regularly. A pace maker is fitted into a person's body during an operation.

Electrical signals

The heart is kept beating by small, electrical signals sent by the brain. Sometimes these signals do not reach the heart. If this happens, the heart may miss a beat. A pace maker is used to make sure that the heart beats in a steady pattern.

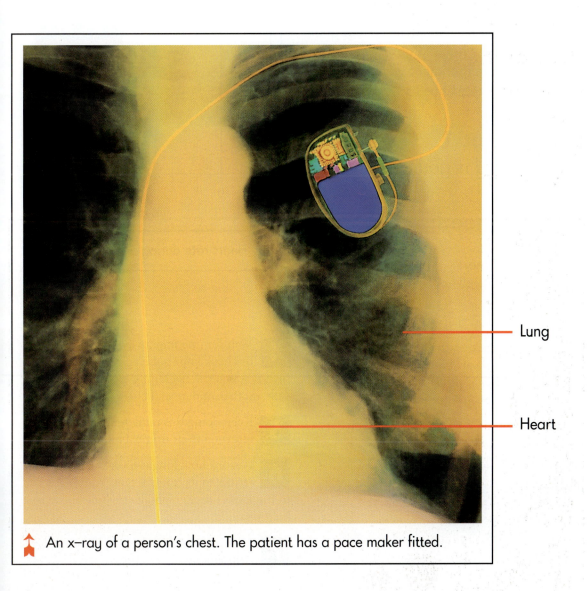

⬆ An x-ray of a person's chest. The patient has a pace maker fitted.

Batteries

Inside a pace maker is a small battery. This sends out extra signals to replace the ones sent by the brain which do not reach the heart. The battery inside the pace maker does not last forever. When the battery runs out, a new battery is fitted during an operation.

9 Experiments

The following two experiments will help you to learn more about how the heart works. The first experiment will help you to work out how healthy your own heart is. The second experiment will show you how hard the heart has to work.

Experiment 1
How healthy is your heart?

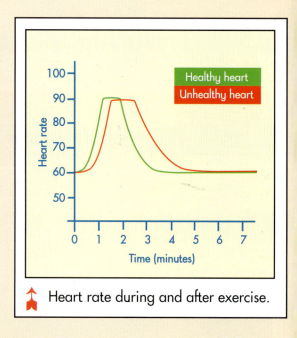

Heart rate during and after exercise.

You will need:
- a stop-watch
- a pair of trainers
- someone to work with.

Method

1 Get your partner to count the number of times your heart beats in 15 seconds by feeling your pulse. Multiply this number of beats by four to give you your normal heart rate.

2 Now run on the spot as hard as you possibly can for two minutes.

3 Get your partner to check your pulse again by counting the number of beats in 15 seconds and multiplying by four. You should find that the pulse rate has increased.

4 Wait for one minute and get your partner to check your pulse again. If it is still faster than it was at the beginning of the experiment, wait another minute and check the pulse again.

5 Keep doing this until your pulse has returned to its original rate.

6 Record how long it took your heart to return to its original rate. You might like to use a table or a graph like the one above to help you.

7 Now swap over and repeat the experiment.

Healthy hearts

The healthier a person's heart is, the quicker it will return to its normal heart rate after having done some physical exercise. In your experiment, the person whose heart rate returned to normal the quickest has the healthier heart. You can improve the health of your heart by taking regular exercise.

Experiment 2
How hard does your heart work?

When resting, your heart pumps about a cup full of blood around your body every time it beats. This means that in one minute, your heart pumps about six litres of blood. To find out how hard this is to do, carry out the following experiment.

You will need:
- two buckets
- a cup
- a litre measure
- lots of water
- a stop-watch
- someone to work with.

Method

1. Measure out six litres of water into one bucket. The other bucket is empty.

2. Get your partner to time one minute whilst you try to move the water from one bucket to the other using the cup. You must be very careful not to spill any water.

3. Check you still have six litres of water. If you haven't, you have not worked as well as a healthy heart which never spills blood.

Glossary

999 — 999 is the number you dial on a telephone when you need the police, the fire brigade, the coastguard or an ambulance in an emergency.

Artery — An artery is a tube which takes blood from the heart to the rest of the body.

Atria — The atria are the top chambers in the heart.

Backbone — The backbone is the bone that goes down your back. The backbone is also called the spine.

Brain — The brain is the part of your body that does all your thinking and controls your body.

Breast plate — The breast plate is another name for the sternum.

Donor card — A donor card is a card carried by people saying that if they die, they are happy for their organs to be taken out of their body and given to other people.

Electrical signals — The brain and the body use electrical signals to send messages to each other.

Heart attack — A heart attack is when the heart stops beating.

Hole in the heart — To have a hole in the heart is when the two top chambers of the heart (called the atria) are connected by a hole.

Involuntary muscle — An involuntary muscle is a muscle that is not consciously controlled by the brain.

Leaky valve — A leaky valve is a valve inside the heart that allows some blood to flow back in the direction it came from.

Lungs — The lungs are the part of our body that take in oxygen and allow us to breathe.

Muscle — A muscle is a part of our body that makes the bones move. Muscles are usually controlled by the brain.

Organ — An organ is a part of the body which has a particular job to do. The heart, lungs, kidneys and liver are organs.

Oxygen — Oxygen is the gas we need to live.

Oxygenated blood — Oxygenated blood is blood that has oxygen in it.

Pace maker — A pace maker is a small, electrical device which is put inside the body to make sure that the heart beats regularly.

Pulse — A pulse is a feeling made when arteries near the surface of the skin throb in time to the heart beating.

Rib cage — The rib cage is the group of bones that are at the front of your chest.

Sternum — The sternum is the name of the bone which goes down the middle of your chest and is joined to the rib cage.

Surgeon — A surgeon is a person who performs operations on the body.

Transplant — A transplant is an operation during which an organ is taken out of the body and changed for a new one.

Vein — A vein is a tube which takes blood from the rest of the body back to the heart.

Ventricles — The ventricles are the bottom chambers in the heart.

Further information

Further reading
The Human Body by H Amery and J Songi, Hamlyn 1993
Blood and Circulation by J Hardie, Heinemann 1996

Places to visit
Human Biology Exhibition, at
Natural History Museum, London
Open: 10.00 a.m. – 6.00 p.m. (Monday to Saturday)
11.00 a.m. – 6.00 p.m. (Sunday)

Science for Life, at
Natural History Galleries, Manchester Museum
Open: 10.00 a.m. – 5.00 p.m. (Monday to Saturday only)

Index

Aa arteries 6, 7, 11, 15
atrium 6, 7

Bb backbone 4, 5
blocked arteries 15
blood 6, 7, 8, 9
breastplate (sternum) 4, 5

Cc chambers 6, 7, 14

Ee exercise 20
experiments 20, 21

Hh heart attack 15, 16
heartbeat 8, 11
hole in the heart 12, 13, 14

Ll leaky valves 12, 13, 14

Mm missing beats 18, 19

Oo oxygen 8, 9

Pp pace maker 18, 19
problems 12, 13, 14
pulse 10, 11
pumps 2, 8, 9, 21

Rr rib cage 4, 5

Ss size 6

Tt transplant 17, 18

Vv valves 6, 12, 13, 14
veins 6, 7
ventricle 6, 7